a A

b B

c C

d D

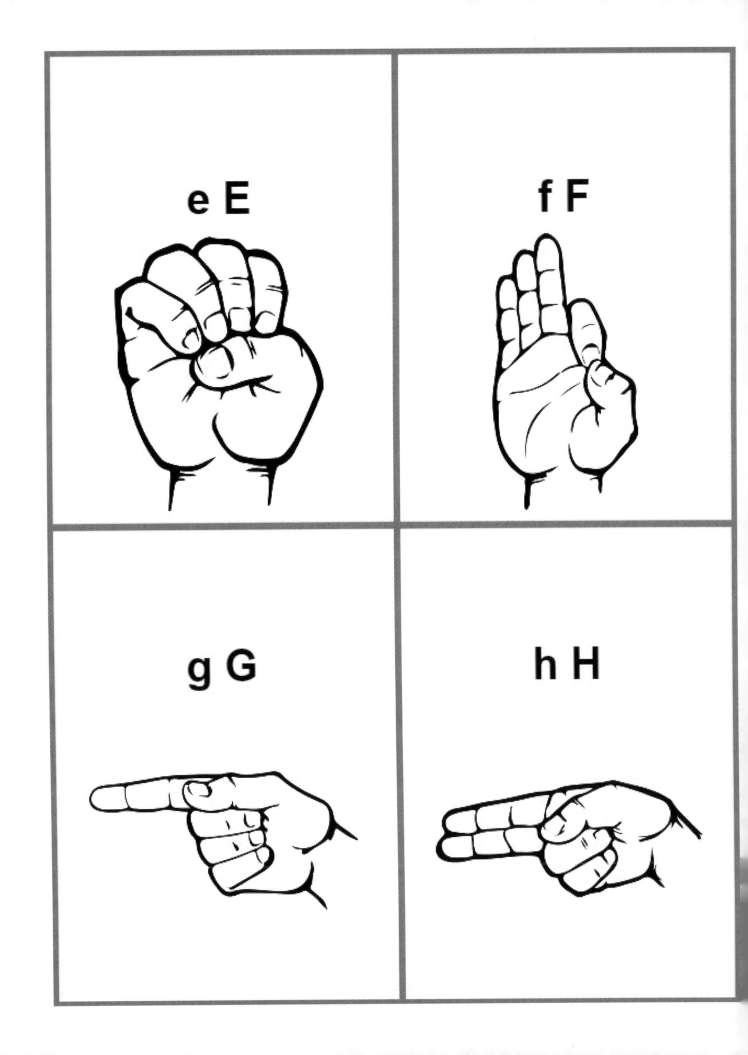

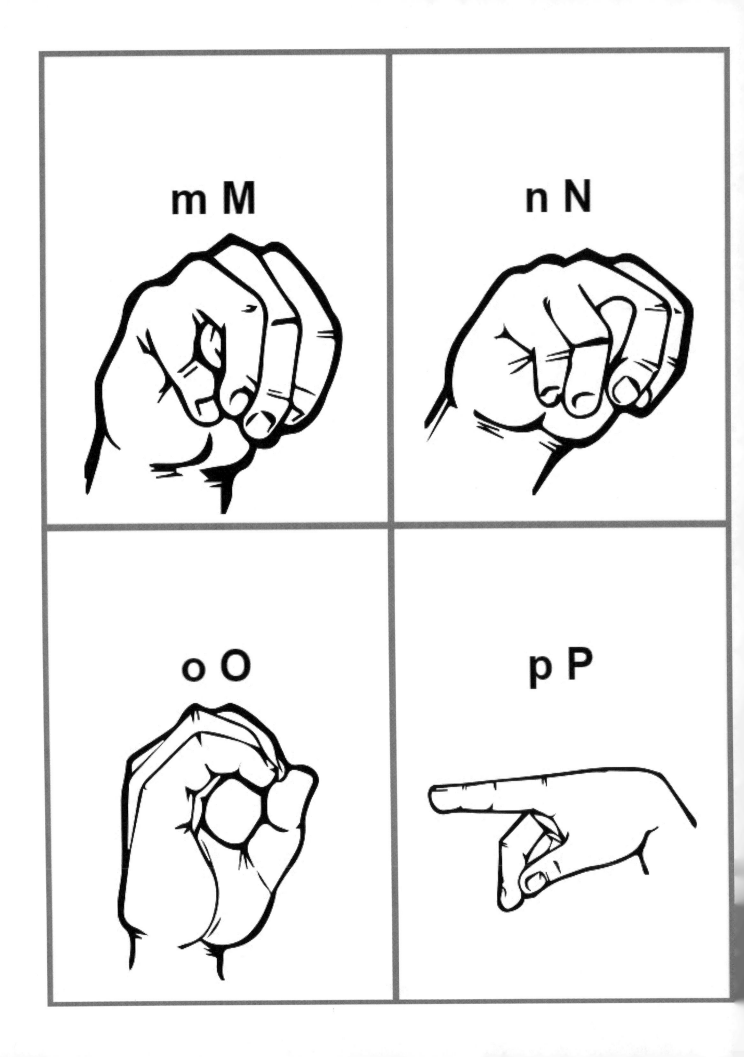

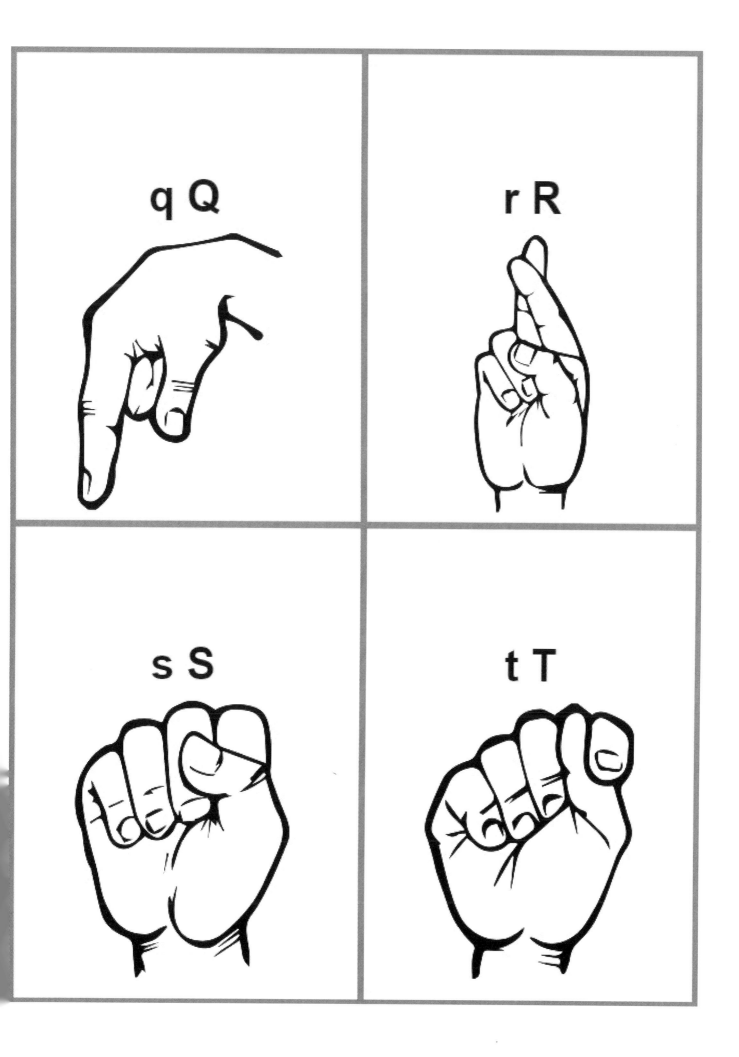

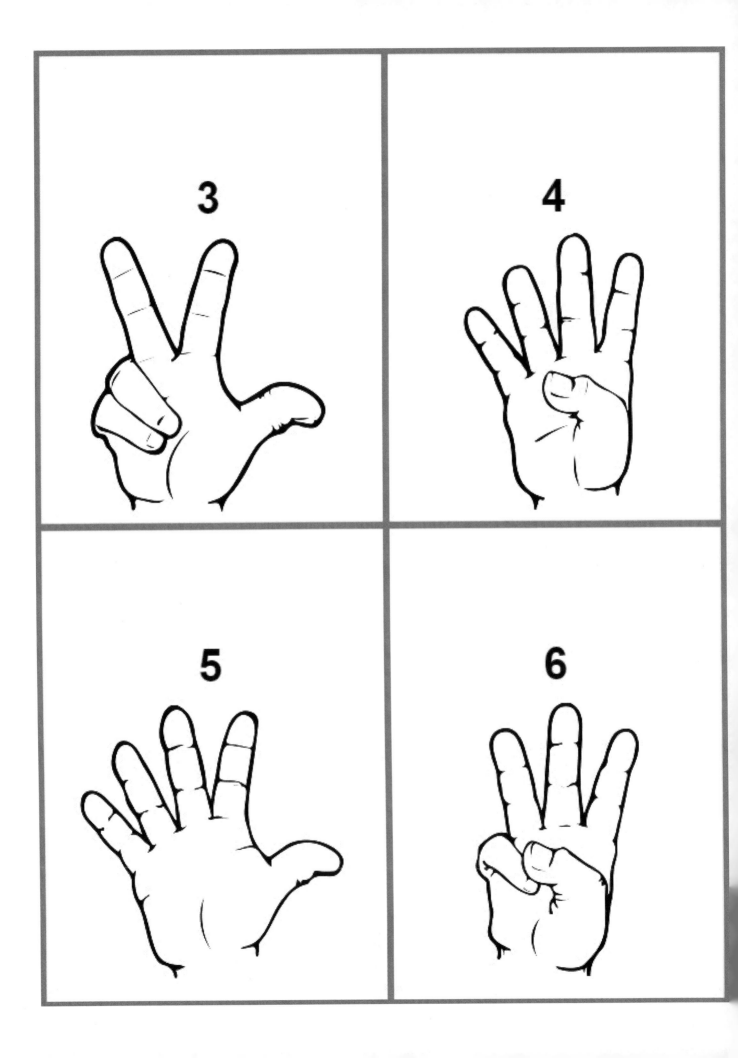

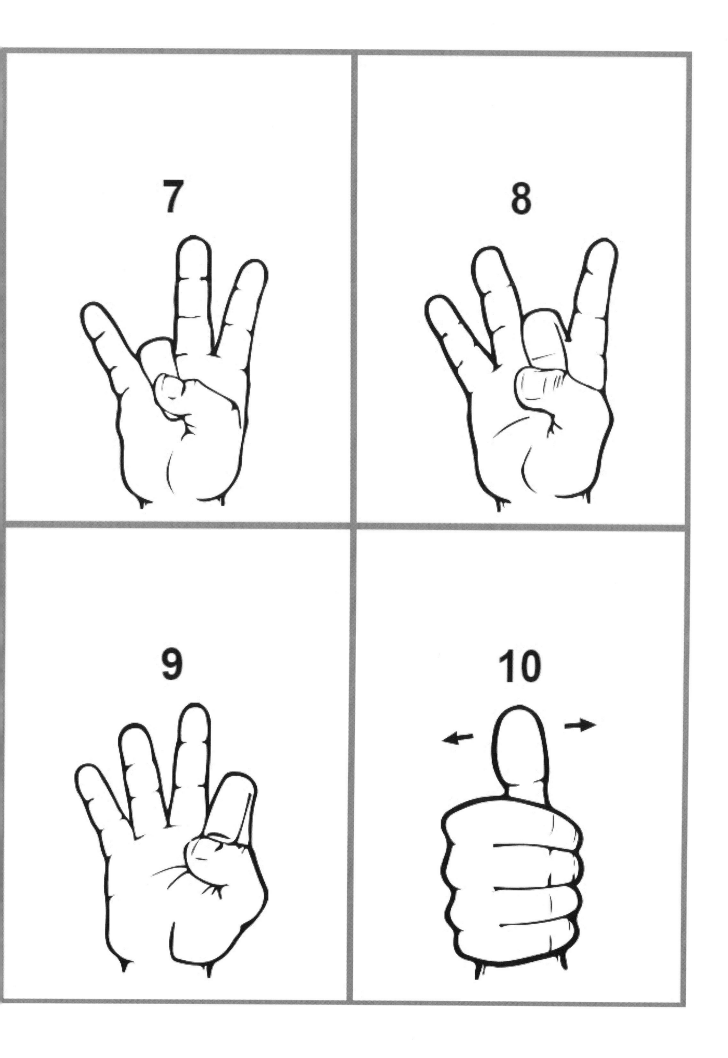

0

who

thumb on chin, bend
index finger twice

what

shrug shoulders, palms
up and out

where

index finger moves side
to side

when cirlcle right index finger over left index finger, then tap	**why** grabber hand touch forehead, then comes down to 'y'
how curved hands touch @ knuckles at chest, face down. flip them	**which** hands as thumbs up, alternate up and down

same 'y' hand slides side to side	**different** pointer fingers make X, then uncross them
wrong 'y' comes up to chin	**ask** pointer finger facing out, move forward and change to x

understand fist at forehead, index finger shoots out	**don't understand** fist at forehead, index finger shoots out while shaking your
help left hand thumbs up, right flat palm comes underneath it	**again** flat left hand with palm up, right hand is flat, taps middle

slow right hand slides up back of left hand	**feel** middle finger swipes up chest multiple times
today 'y' hands down twice	**now** 'y' hands down ONCE

tired cupped hands with fingertips on chest, curve hands down so s	**stressed** flat left hand pushes down right fist. blow out air, facial
sad palms towards face, drag hands down length of face. tilt hea	**happy** opens palms to chest, two up and circular motions

puzzled

point forward, bring hand up and change it to 'x' letter sig

relieved

right arm above left arm, move both down and blow air out

satisfied

right arm above left arm, tap torso ONCE

mischievious

'3' sign at sides of head, bend fingers in and out

nice right hand slides down palm of left hand	**sleep** open palm at top of face, slide down to a grabber hand
sick tap head and stomach with middle fingers	**sympathy / poor you** open hands with middle finger bent slightly, forward circles

early

middle right finger slides across back of left hand

late

arm bent to side, hand flips back towards self

negative

flat left palm raised up, side of right index finger hits le

not/dont

flick thumb from bottom of chin, shake head, furrow brows

busy	home
right hand 'b' sways side to side next to left hand fist	grabber hand taps next to mouth, then up higher on cheek
work	**homework**
right fist taps down on side of left fist twice	right grabber hand taps cheek, then forms fist and taps side

hard

double 'x' hands, right one comes down on left twice

easy

palms up, right hand flicks left fingers from bottom

start

flat left palm facing sideways, right index finger twist in

word

left hand points up, right hand as 'g' taps tip of left inde

many	much/a lot
grabber hands facing up, open ONCE	clawed hands facing each other but apart, then pull even fur
more	everyday
grabber hands tap fingertips	right hand thumbs up, rub knuckles across cheek twice

want open hands facing up, pull towards chest and make claws	**don't want** open hands, facing up, pull towards chest and make claws, fl
first (counting) left hand thumbs up, right index finger taps thumg	**first (place)** right index finger swipes facing out, them turns in towards

middle

flat left palm up, flat right hand swivel then hit left palm

last

pinkies out, right one hits down on left one

facial expression

'L' next to head, alternate up and down

try

thumbs up, facing self, then turn down and out, swooping pal

use left hand flat, palm down, right hand 'u' shape making up an	**need** 'x' letter makes little strikes, mouth as if saying 'eee'
ought to 'x' letter makes little strikes, mouth as if saying 'aaah'	**should** 'x' letter makes little strikes, mouth as if saying 'ooooh'

must 'x' letter upright, then tilt down once. mouth as if saying	**never** right hand flat, makes a question mark like motion in air
each thumbs up, right hand moves down behind left hand	**eyes** point to each eye

see

'k' letter sign, palm facing you, hold near eyes and move fo

finish

open hands with palms facing self, swing out so palms face o

fingerspelling

wiggle fingers with palm facing down, move hand across chest

teach

grabber hands pointed to sides of head, move forward twice

college

left hand flat palm face self, right flat hand palm face out

dorm

'd' letter sign taps near mouth, then higher up cheek

party

swinging 'y' hands or swinging 'p' hands

fun

'u' letter with left hand facing down, 'u' with right hand t

read

left hand flat palm up,
right two fingers 'read'
left hand

lie

flat hand palm down
slides across mouth
from left to right

guess

'c' across forehead first
open, them close

near

left hand bent in, right
hand also bent in, but
hits inside

partner

left flat hand palm face self, flat right hand sweeps over l

dead

right hand up, left down, them switch

fine

open hand, tap thumb on chest

fish

flat hand swims forward

same old	confused
'y' hands circles by sides	tap head, circular motions with hands, right over left
boring	**walk (3)**
index finger tap side of nose, twist hand outward	hands flap, mimic walking '3' slide forward and backwalk with

talk (deaf) (2) hands shake by sides'c' hands claw air	**talk (hearing)** '4' taps chin
wake up closed 'L' to open next to eyes, widen eyes and raise eyebro	**hearing** index finger makes forward circles infront of mouth, show te

deaf tap near ear, tap near mouth	**watch tv** 'v' sign pointing forward, slides forward from side of eyes.
play ball twist 'y' hands at sidesmake ball with cupped hands	**time** tap wrist with 'x' letter hand

tell me tap chin, tap chest	**what does it mean** flat left hand, palm up. right two fingers tap palm, make ci
oh i see 'i' letter sign, slanted up and down	**look at me** 'v' pointing out, then turn on self

focus flat hands at side of face move forward	**ready** 'r' letter signs move left to right
know tap forehead	**don't know** tap forehead, then twist hand out. shake head

bed hands to side of face like a pillow	**system** fists with thumbs touching, move out to create half a box
nothing / not much grabber hands start next to each other, then slide away from	**so-so** flat palm facing down swing back and fourth

later 'I' letter sign tilt out towards side	**study** left palm flat, up. right hand wiggles fingers over it.
quiz spelled out fast so looks like a sign	**test** question marks in the air

exam question marks in the air, with exploding dots at the end	**how many** palms up, them move up and open. furrow brows
sentences F hand shapes, index and thumbs tap, then wiggle hands apart	**class** C hands, palms face out, then swoop around in circular motion, facing self

tutor T hands shake near sides	**not yet** later (arm bent at side, hand swings backwards) with tongue out slightly
office O hands, arms bend in front, right in front of left, then straighten both out	**father** open hand, thumb taps forhead

children palm down, tap two kids heads	**free** F hands crossed at wrist, palms face in. swoop to uncross and face outward
what did you do? (do-do) open/close L hands, palms facing up	**computer** C hand taps up and down arm

bad	play
hand at mouth, turn to face down and move away from mouth	Y hands twist back and fourth at sides
remember	**other**
thumbs up, right thumb taps forehead then taps top of other thumb	thumb up, moves sideways once (like ten, but once)

movement grabber hands face down, slide both up like S shape	**half** index finger out, move hand down and left middle finger come out
forget wipe R hand across forhead	**a lot** hands open and close, then move outward in circular motion

favorite	before
tap chin with middle finger	wave hand up/down next to head, hand points backwards
right	**to get better**
index fingers up, right hand fist comes down on left	side of right hand taps up left arm

can't

right index finger hits down on left index finger, palms facing down

complain

C hand sideways and facing self, taps chest

excuse

left hand palm up, right hand rubs fingertips along length of pinky twice

game

thumbs up, tap knuckles

tie T hands, touching thumbs, pull hands apart	**yesterday** A letter hand with palm facing out taps side of chin, then near ear
past wave hand pointing backwards ONCE next to side of head	**will** flat hand, palm facing left and up near forehead, tilt down and forward

introduce	meet
flat hands facing up scoop near belly to come together	both index fingers up, hands come together
go	water
both index fingers up, move forward and tilt fingers towards a direction	W hand, touch index finger to mouth twice

tea left hand as sideways O, right hand as F, index and thumb fingertips inside the O	**coffee** left fist on side, right fist over it on side as well, right fist moves in circles
make out hands as fists, crossed at wrists, both fists move up and down	**dream** tap forehead with index finger, pull hand up and bend finger into letter X

stuck

V hand fingertips touch throat

roommate

claw like hands facing self, interlock fingers twice

complicated

X hands face eachother, then move in towards eachother

new

cupped hands facing up, back right hand skims inside of left hand

hard of hearing U hand, pointing out slightly to side, then move arm to point forward	**bathroom** one T hand shakes side to side
football hands leaning in towards eachother, upright, interlock fingers twice	**rest** make x with arms over chest, open hands

random

confused sign, moves across chest

fix

grabber hands face each other, alternate moving them up and down

dunkin donuts

D hand move forward, then move over slightly and move forward again

support

left fist comes up under right fist with thumb up

lose V hand swipes from bottom of left palm up to fingertips	**love it** fist at mouth with palm facing out, move fist forward
president claw hands at sides of head, move hands apart and close into fists	**stop** right hand down sideways on left flat hand palm up

sometimes

index finger faces self scoops towards self in left palm that faces up

donut

make a circle with index + middle fingers and thumbs

store

push shopping cart with grabber hands facing down, up near face

restaurant

R hand moves from right to left across mouth

daughter

B hand face down
(salute from chin),
move hand to crook of
left arm

son

B hand face down
(salute from forehead),
move hand to crook of
left arm

some

left hand palm up, right
hand flat palm in slice
down width of hand

move

grabber hands face
down, lift up from one
spot and move to
another

wonder

index finger face forehead, make small circles

hear / listen

alien hand (3 hand) at hear, bend fingers in and out

upset

C hand facing self taps stomach

depressed

loose hand with bent middle finger, moves down chest. sad face

angry	hungry
claw hands at stomach, pull hands up and out towards sides. mad face	C hand faces chest, move from top of chest to bottom
visual	breakfast
V hands face self, make small circles that alternate, infront of eyes	eat + morning

cereal palm face towards self, slightly up. small scoop motions towards self	**voice** V hand moves up/down neck
stay Y hands facing down, move hands down	**equal** have hands tap fingertips

fair

hand hands with thumbs up tap fingertips

draw / art

left hand flat facing right, right pinky draws down left hand's palm

bother / annoy

right flat hand hit in crook of left thumb and index finger

wonderful

flat hands face out at sides of head, move hands out and down, mouth makes "O"

dialogue D hands alternate moving back and fourth	**follow** index fingers up, right hand in front of left, move and tilt both forward
both right hand makes 2, slide down width of left palm	**lazy** L hand hits left side of chest, palm faces in

family

F hands circle around so sides of pinkies touch

don't have

have hands tap chest, shake head

i missed it

fist moves towards back of head at side of head. index comes out.

chesmitry

C hands alternating circles towards self

biology

B hands alternating circles towards self

math

M hands, right comes down on left wrist

eggs

U hands, right fingertips come down on left. both move down and apart

absent

slight bent middle finger on left hand, hit finger with right index

problem

double 'X' hands hit knuckles alternate up and down.

tough

double 'X' hands hit knuckles once.

difficulty

double 'X' hands tap knuckles, twists forward and back

make

right fist on top of left, twist back and fourth like grinding pepper

furious claw hands at chest, pull up and apart. furrow brows. strong facial expression	**exhausted** tired with strong facial expression
enjoy / joyful please with both hands	**overwhelmed** hands move back past head. facial expression

enthusiastic / eager

rub hands together. happy facial expression

dog

The right hand pats the right knee, and then the fingers are snapped.

both of us, three of us, etc.

'V' with palm up, directional. points to people involved

doesn't matter

flat hands facing self. right hand hits left fingertips, forward and back

warning	none
warning	**none**
left fist face down, right hand hits top of fist	'O' hands together up at chest, move outward from each other once. shake head.

nothing	heavy
nothing	**heavy**
'O' hands toward and away from each other.	both hands out, palms up. move down, up, down, up.

table (desk) right arm bent over left	**table** 'T' hands make half box
old upside down 'C' hand at chin, pull down slightly and turn into fist	**to grab** left hand flat, right hand scoops at hand

to give to

right grabber hand, lift and move arm forward

pen/pencil

pincher hand at mouth, bring down to flat left hand, move across hand.

sure

index finger at chin, move out and down

what does it mean?

left palm flat, face right. in/up circles with right hand as 'V'. sign 'what'

explain

thumbs to index, fingers out. alternate moving hands in and out

to be clear

grabber hands tap fingertips. move apart, open hands and turn to face palm outward

excuse me

right hand rubs up length of left hand

not / don't / doesn't

thumb up hand flicks thumb under chin

to be unclear hands face each other. make small circles. left in/up right out/down	**to correct / grade** write x on left palm with finger
to erase 'X' rubs on left palm	**to pass out** grabber hand right moves out from left

paper	**student**
rub right hand over left	learn + person
teacher	**with**
teach + person	thumbs up, palms face self. knuckles tap

temple 'T' taps wrist	**church** 'C' taps wrist
take it easy flat hands face down, move over each other and back out	**day** index finger up, move arm down over left

all day

palm open, move arm
down over left

week

index finger up, rub
right knuckles along left
palm

great

both hands open, face
forward next to face.
move back and fourth.
smile

meaning

'V' hand taps left palm
that faces right. twist V
hand and tap again

mean

hands swipe past each other (up and down) then close to fists

disappointed

tap chin with index finger. sad face. mouth 'ooo'

disgusted

claw hand on chest, make small circles. grossed out facial expression.

halloween

peek a boo hands over face than open then close

our 'B' hand scoops from right shoulder around chest to left.	**candy** index on cheek, twist back and fourth
cat pull at whiskers	**break (something)** fists touch at sides, bend both out and apart

buy rub grabber hand from bottom of hands off finger tips	**flatter** right hand hits fingertips back and fourth on left index finger
philosophy 'K' hand makes small circles at forhead	**highschool** sign H then S

high 'H' hand moves up	**history** 'H' hand shakes up and down
heard of hearing 'H' hand moves from chin down, then up over and down once more	**psychology** left hand makes a non asl u, right flat hand taps in crook of left thumb

cleaning

rub right hand on left palm up to fingertips multiples times

weird

'W' hand moves across mouth, fingers bend in and out

english

right hand covers left hand as fist facing down, or as flat hand facing down

luck

tough slight bent middle to mouth, turn hand outwards

expensive grabber right hand on flat left facing up, grab and move up and off hand	**purse** have hand tucks in armpit
king 'K' hand moves from top of chest diagonally down	**window** flat hands face in, right on left. move hand up or down to mean open or close

contacts tap at each eye with slight bent middle	**twice** 'V' hand palm up flicks up palm of flat hand facing right
manchester 'M' hand twists at wrist	**insurance** 'I' hand moves side to side

grocery store / super market eat + store	**cheese** heel of hands wist back and fourth on each other multiple times
milk thumbs up, rub front of fingers up/down (palms face eachother)	**butter** '3' hand but middle and index together. swipe down width of left hand's palm

cook flat hands, right on left - palm down. flip over so palm is up.	**hartford** H hand moves up and down, with arm across chest
hospital H taps right side of forehead, then left side	**team** T hands tap at thumbs, make outward circle

project K hand with palm down, pinky down the back of hand (hand stays in)	**banquet** grabber hands make inward circles that alternate (like sign)
100 '1' then 'C'	**celebration / anniversary** 'A' hands make inward circles (at the same time) at side s of head

wait

left hand in front of right, wiggle fingers (palms up, slightly towards self)

lecture

arm up right at side of head, twist hand side to side at wrist

geography / earth

thumb and middle on back of left hand. tilt right hand forward and back

sociology

'S' hands circle outward

physics double x hands. fingers intersect multiple times (hard hands)	**because** middle finger flap up and down at side of head. eyebrows raised
every week sign week multiple times	**hurt** index fingers point at each other, palms in. don't touch

science thumbs down - palms out. cirles towards self, alternating	**fuel / gasoline** left hand is 'O' on side, right fist with thumb up, put thumb in O
interesting 'like' with both hands	**hurry** both 'H' hands move up and down at wrist

statistics 'work' but right hand makes small swoops over left. doesn't tap it.	**major** 'B' hands face each other. right on left, slide forward
take 'lights off' with both hands, but lower.	**all** 'A' hand, slide over and change to 'L'

birthday flat hands on chest, move out to face up	**last week** 'week' and 'before'
next week 'next' and 'week'	**medicine** middle finger taps left palm

presentation both hands up and out, right in front of left	**internship** left hand as fist palm down, 'i' hand at side of fist, swipe forward and back
linguistics 'L' hands touch at thumb, move apart and close to fists	**live** thumbs up, move up chest

semester

'S' hand across body starting at left side, them move down

trouble

'B' hands tilted in slightly make crossing circles in front of face

can

fists up at top of chest, simply move fists down

patient

thumb up at chin with knuckles out (palm faces left). pull thumb nail down chin

silly 'Y' hand (just one) twists back and fourth at wrist	**foolish** two 'Y' hands, right in front of left (both in front of face) small circles
drop opposite of take	**ocean** loose open hands, palms down. move both to mimic waves.

visit

V hands make outward alternating circles up at eyes

big headed

make C's with index and thumbs. at sides of face. facial expression, showing teeth.

of course / normal

N hand with fingers pointing outward. swivel and hit outside of wrist.

infection

i hand moves side to side

india

thumb up hand, thumb taps forehead with fist in air.

europe

E hand faces forehead, makes small cirlcles

example

tap with index at flat left palm, facing right.

cool

twist fist with index knuckle out slightly at cheek

people K hands make small outward circles that alternate at chest	**wear** flat hands facing chest, swoop down and out like try
group G hands make outward circle, like family	**event** swipe up chest with slight bent middle fingers, no facial expression

what's up

swipe up chest with slight bent middle fingers, furrowed brows

thanksgiving

G hand moves from chin down. faces up or down

city

flat hands face each other at angle, slide fingertips back and forth.

town

flat hands face each other at angle, tap fingertips

insult index points forward, move forward and twist wrist to move index facing up	**character** C hand makes outward circle on left side of chest, then tap chest once
look like index up, taps cheek then change to Y hand, shake back and forth	**identity** I hand taps thumb side to palm facing forward of left hand

choice

pick at fingertips of 5 hand

catch

open hands together at pinky sides, palms up. out from chest, pull in.

location

flat hands, palms down. left up over right, right taps down multiple times

corner

make corner with flat hands on sides

across

touch index fingertips,
pull apart

intersection

make a cross with index
fingers

highway

index fingers point past
each other in opposite
directions

black

wipe index finger
across forhead

red

pull index finger down from chin, change finger to a hook

orange

squeeze hand at front of chin multiple times

yellow

Y hand twists back and forth

blue

B hand twists side to side

green

G hand twists side to side

purple

P hand twists side to side

pink

V hand with middle finger on chin, pull hand down

white

open hand at chest, pull hand out and close

brown B hand slides down cheek	**tan** T hand slides down cheek
gold tap cheek with index, pull down to Y and shake	**silver** tap cheek with index, pull down to fist and shake

off point

index fingers pointing
out together at thumbs,
move right hand
forward and to side

snow

claw hands come down
from sky

rain

fingertips come down
from sky

snow shoes

snow + fists with
thumbs down tap at
thumbs

sun c hand moves out from head, turn back to self and open (like rays)	**iceskate** X hands swing side to side, palms facing up
rollerblade double X hands swing side to side, face down	**blazer** B hands face e/o, swing side to side

capital / governor point index finger out, curve index to self, tap forehead	**korea** hand wipes down face, tap side of forehead
topic/title U hands bend to double X, turn to face eachother	**cookies** C hand facing down on palm, tap + twist, tap. multiple

email

C hand, flat hand cuts through opening

pick on

X hand rub on back of index finger multiple

missing

W slides down from closed hand

disappear

index down from open hand (index between fingers of hand)

let them know / inform grabber hands move out from head	**still** Y hands arch from stomach up/out
thing flat hand palm up at chest, move over	**object** claw hand taps chest

hockey upside down X hand on palm up, move X over twice	**crazy** c hand makes circles at side of face
olympic O hands that interlock, flip over and interlock again	**fall** flat palm wipes down at elbow, left arm is bent up at elbow, towards self

winter cold with no facial expression	**spring** hand comes up/out of C hand on side
summer index finger wipes across forehead, turn to hook	**drunk** thumb up wipes across mouth with thumb pointing left

broke up fists together at thumb, pull apart and down, plus U-P	**kill** hand flat palm down, right hand with index stabbing under flat hand
drama thumbs up, make alternating inward circles at chest	**way** flat hands face e/o, move forward

street	address
arms down at sides, swing forward	'live' but multiple times
phone	**relay service**
Y at ear, with thumb at ear and pinky at mouth	R hands cross each other

Made in the USA
Middletown, DE
31 January 2024

48860574R00060